DEDICATED TO MY SON...

I Dedicate This Series To Jason, My Incredibly Gifted Son, Who Has The Most Remarkable Kind And Gentle Spirit..!

Jason

Unless otherwise indicated, all Scripture quotations are taken from the King James Version of the Bible.

#DearSon, Volume 1 / ISBN 10: 1-56394-441-3 / ISBN 13: 978-1563944413 / B-299

Copyright © 2010 by **MIKE MURDOCK**

Publisher/Editor: Deborah Murdock Johnson

Published by The Wisdom Center · 4051 Denton Hwy. · Ft. Worth, Texas 76117

1-817-759-BOOK · 1-817-759-2665 · 1-817-759-0300

You Will Love Our Website..! WisdomOnline.com

www.twitter.com/DrMikeMurdock

WHY I WROTE THIS BOOK

I Love My Son..!

As I have become involved with "Twitter" I have discovered a new outlet for sharing Twisdom Keys *immediately*...as The Holy Spirit brings them to my mind.

I have been having wonderful thoughts toward my son. From these thoughts my #**DearSon** "Tweets" are birthed. Because of my strong love and affection for my son, he is very *important* to me. I also feel *very protective* over him. These "Tweets" to my precious son are from the heart of a loving father. I think every son would love for his father to give him such vital *insight* about building a strong relationship with that *special* person in his life.

"Tweeting" has become a rewarding way to express my opinions and counsel to my son and many others who enjoy being mentored through my #**DearSon** Twisdom Keys. It transcends *time* and *place*...no matter where I am or what time of the day...I can share with you what is burning on my heart at that very moment.

Allow these Twisdom Keys to enter your Mind. They will *inspire* and *motivate* you to discover the Art of *Receiving* what God has intended for you.

That is why I wrote this book.

Mike Murdock

SON1 #DearSon
Some #People Are Just #*Contentious*,
Uncomfortable With #Peace,
Restless In An Environment of #Order.
#Dad@64.
#drMM

SON2 #DearSon
#Delilah...Views You
As A Mountain To Be *Conquered*.
Proverbs 31 Woman...Views You
As A *Jewel* To Be Protected.
#drMM

SON3 #DearSon
EVERYTHING...Has A *Price*.
(#Pleasure. #Friendships. Info.)
Price...Never Indicates #*Value*.
Never.
#Dad@64.
#drMM

SON4 #DearSon
Some Will Use Kind #Words...
Like Tools/*Bait*.
Some ARE #Kind...*Exploring*.
#Time *Exposes* Their #Difference.
#drMM

SON5 #DearSon
#Beauty Is...The Part You SEE.
#Ugly Is...The Part You Don't.

Never Forget It, Son.
#drMM

`SON6` #DearSon
Some...*Need* You.
Few...*Heed* You.
One...#*Believes* You.
The #Decision Is Made For You.
#drMM

`SON7` #DearSon
#God Keeps An #Esther...*Waiting*
In The *Wings.*
Always.
#drMM

`SON8` #DearSon
You And Her Are In #Love
With...The *Same* Person.
Her.
#drMM

`SON9` #DearSon
A #Wife Cannot Solve
All Your #Problems.
But, She Better Be Able
To Solve...*More* Than One.
Dad.
#drMM

`SON10` #DearSon
Her #*Reactions* To You...

Reveal Her *#Understanding* of You.
Her Understanding...
Decides Her #Future With You.
#drMM

SON11 #DearSon
The #Decision Is Not Hard.
#The_Right_One Is...The One You
#Love To *Talk* To The Most.
#drMM

SON12 #DearSon
#The_*Right*_One Is A #Burden_Bearer,
...Not A Burden.
Is Your Load Heavier or *Easier*...
Since She Entered Your #Life?
#drMM

SON13 #DearSon
Watch Her #Work.
Her #Productivity Will *Explain* Her.
(Rebekah/Ruth/Proverbs 31)
#Beauty Is The *Door*~Not The House.
#drMM

SON14 #DearSon
When Does SHE Enjoy You Most?
When You Are *#Strong*/#*Weak*?
When Do YOU #Enjoy *Her* Most?
When She Is *Strong/Weak*?
#drMM

SON15 #DearSon
No #Woman Is...*Unaware* of Herself,
Nor Her *Impact.*
#drMM

SON16 #DearSon
Do You Really Want A #Woman
Who Doesn't #Trust Your #*Decisions?*
Leave Her For The #*Fool* Who Does.
#drMM

SON17 #DearSon
#The_Right_One...Will *Unleash* #Energy
To TALK Your Highest #Thoughts.
Unceasingly.
(#Disinterest *Reveals.*)
#drMM

SON18 #DearSon
Her #*Disinterest* In Your #Responsibilities...
IS Your Answer.
(#Burden_*Bearer*...or *Burden?*)
#Dad@64.
#drMM

SON19 #DearSon
Her #*Reactions*...Will Be A *Fragrance*
...or An *Odor.*
(Making Your #Decision *Easy.*)
#drMM

SON20 #DearSon
How *Attentive* Is She To Your~
...#Responsibilities?
...#Achievements?
...#Preferences?
...#Comfort?
...Silence?
Dad.
#drMM

SON21 #DearSon
If She Will Not *#Listen*...
She Will *Never* Become.
(Your #Words *Matter*...or They *Don't*.)
#drMM

SON22 #DearSon
If She Is Unhappy...
Working With You~
She Would Be #Unhappy...
Living With You.
#Dad@64.
#drMM

SON23 #DearSon
Test.
Test.
Make *"Small"* Requests.
Her #Reaction Is...Your #Answer.
Accept It. Save Your #Life
...And *Hers*.
#drMM

SON24 #DearSon
#The_Right_One...
Will Not *Resent* How
You Want To *Spend* Your #Time.
#drMM

SON25 #DearSon
Women POSE...To Say The *Unspoken*.
(Yes, Even On #Twitter.)
(Smile...)
#drMM

SON26 #DearSon
Prodigal Son~Lost Father's #Blessing
...Thru #Dishonor.
Absalom~Lost #Father's Blessing
...Thru #Dishonor.
Be Careful.
#drMM

SON27 #DearSon
A *Moment* of #Loneliness...
Can Birth A *Lifetime* of #Pain.
#drMM

SON28 #DearSon
Interesting Women...Are Plentiful.
An Assigned #Woman Is...The *Rare* One.
She Is Your..."*Nest Without Thorns.*"
#drMM

SON29 #DearSon
Two Kinds of #Mates:
One~Wants You To Be Pleasured By
...Whatever *She* Does.
One~Wants To Do Whatever
Pleasures *You*.
#drMM

SON30 #DearSon
Those Comfortable In The *Bedroom*
May Not Be Comfortable In The *#Prayer* Room.
#drMM

SON31 #DearSon
Does She *Increase*...or *Decrease* Your Load?
Is Her #Priority To Understand YOU...or Be
Understood?
Honestly.
#drMM

SON32 #DearSon
A *Bitter* #Woman Is...A Sad Experience...
And, No *#MAN* Can Cure Her.
(*Only* #God.)
#drMM

SON33 #DearSon
You Will Not Be The Reason She #Submits To You;
It Will Be Fruit of The #God_Nature Within Her.
(Not Your Burden.)
#drMM

`SON34` #DearSon
She May Want You...
But *Not* Your #Future.
She May Want Your *Future*...
But Not You.
#The_*Right*_One Will Want...*Both.*
#drMM

`SON35` #DearSon
The #Woman In Your *Face*...
Will Never *Walk* By Your Side.
#drMM

`SON36` #DearSon
If She Does Not #*DISCERN* You...
She Has Not *EARNED* You.
#drMM

`SON37` #DearSon
{Never Cut In Line}
~It Reveals Contempt For Others And
~Exposes Unspeakable #*Pride.*
Self-Absorption Is Sad.
#drMM

`SON38` #DearSon
I Don't Judge A #Woman By *Beauty.*
Too Many Varieties/Self-Absorption.
I Judge...By Her #*Ability* To Motivate Me.
#drMM

SON39 #DearSon
The *Accusatory* Mouth...Reveals
A #Heart of *Dishonor.*
Jesus Taught:
Withdraw From House of #Dishonor.
So, Do It.
#drMM

SON40 #DearSon
Her Vocabulary Is That of A...#*Predator.*
That Makes *You*...Her Prey.
Captivity Is...The #Enemy of #Love.
#drMM

SON41 #DearSon
#Delilah Was Not Samson's *Deadliest* #Mistake.
Rejecting His Father's Counsel Was.
#Rebellion Is...An Act of #*Fools.*
#drMM

SON42 #DearSon
Of Course, There's #*Deliverance*
From Her Arrogance, Son.
Bring Her On Vacation To...*Brazil.*
(Smile.)
#drMM

SON43 #DearSon
Kitten #Eyes
But Tiger #*Heart*
Promises Rainbows
Tearing Your #Mind Apart.

(MM Song On Proverbs 7.)
#drMM

SON44 #DearSon
If Her Rage *#Dethrones* You...
You Are Not Ready To Be *#King.*
#drMM

SON45 #DearSon
No #Woman Ever *Follows* A #Man...
She Can *#Deceive.*
Ever.
#drMM

SON46 #DearSon
If Her *#Beauty* Has Made Her
...A Skilled #Receiver
She Will Probably Never Develop
...The *#Nature* of A #Giver.
#drMM

SON47 #DearSon
Know Their *#History.*
History Has A Clear Voice...And Never *Lies.*
#drMM

SON48 #DearSon
A Master *#Listener...*
With The *Right* #Questions
Can *Ignite* That Spark of *#Desire* Within You...
Into A *Raging* Fire.
#drMM

SON49 #DearSon
Don't Use Your #Palace To *Attract* A #Queen;
You Will Always Wonder If She Really #Loves
You...
or The #*Palace.*
#drMM

SON50 #DearSon
Make *Quality*...Your #QUEST.
Incidentally, Neiman-Marcus
Did Not Build *Next* To Wal-Mart.
#drMM

SON51 #DearSon
You Just Know
You'll Want To Discuss Everything With Her.
Everything, Son.
E-V-E-R-Y-T-H-I-N-G.
Dad.
#drMM

SON52 #DearSon
Attempting To Do Something *RIGHT*...
Will Fulfill You Far More Than Attempting To
Do...
Something *Great.*
#drMM

SON53 #DearSon
If She Is Not Captivated
By *What* Has Captivated You
~She Will Eventually #Hate *You* For Loving It.

www.twitter.com/DrMikeMurdock

Believe Me.
#drMM

SON54 #DearSon
Everything You Write...Will Be Read.
...By A *#Friend,* or
...By An *#Enemy.*
Never Forget It, Son.
#drMM

SON55 #DearSon
If She Has Been *Comfortable* With #Liars
...She Will Never Be Comfortable With You.
(*Weaknesses* Are *Trade-Offs.*)
#drMM

SON56 #DearSon
Find *Inexpensive* #Desires.
You Can Experience Them Far *More* Often.
...With *Fewer* Regrets.
#Dad@64.
#drMM

SON57 #DearSon
Beautiful Eyes...And Kind Eyes
Are Very *Different* Messages.
Your *#Heart* Will Explain.
#drMM

SON58 #DearSon
#The_Right_One...
Will *Immerse* Herself In Your #Goals...

If She Has Discerned You
As Her #*Divine* Assignment. (Ruth)
#drMM

SON59 #DearSon
#*Beauty* Is...The Door.
But~It Is NOT The House.
Lots Inside, Son.
Lingering Too Long At Door...Often *Blinds*.
#drMM

SON60 #DearSon
Marry A #Woman Whose Opinion Greatly
Matters To You.
A #*Decision*-Maker.
Insist On Her *Feedback*.
Hidden Gold.
#drMM

SON61 #DearSon
Study Her #*Reactions:*
...To Your *Accomplishments*.
...To Your *Preference* List.
...To Your #*Schedule*.
...To Her *Mother*.
#drMM

SON62 #DearSon
#The_Right_One
...Would Rather *Hear* Your Voice
   Than Stay Asleep.

...Will Not *Embarrass* You
...*Studies* You.
#drMM

SON63 #DearSon
Loneliness...Makes #Delilah Look Like A
Proverbs 31 #Woman.
Loneliness Is *Devastating* To Your #Judgment,
Son.
#drMM

SON64 #DearSon
If She Is Capable of *Deceiving* You...
It Becomes Impossible For Her To #*Follow* You.
(No Admiration.)
#drMM

SON65 #DearSon
It's *Natural* To Want To Take Care of Her.
Unfortunately, She Could Expect You To *Become*
Daddy
And Never *Return* The Care-Giving.
#drMM

SON66 #DearSon
When Someone Forces You To #*Defend* Yourself,
You Are Being
#Attacked.
Only An #*Adversary*...Attacks.
#Dad@64.
#drMM

SON67 #DearSon
Warning Signs:
...A *#Past* She Won't Discuss
...*#Money* She Didn't Earn
...*#Debts* She Can't Pay
...*House* She Won't Clean.
#drMM

SON68 #DearSon
#The_Right_One
...Won't Ask Inappropriate #Questions
...Attempt *"Control* By Contact"
...Evade Direct Questions.
#drMM

SON69 #DearSon
She Will Be Your #Heaven
...or She Will Be Your #Hell.
Listen To The #Spirit
...The Spirit Always Tells.
Dad.
#drMM

SON70 #DearSon
She Is The Costliest *#Investment* of Your
#Lifetime.
Your #Heaven...or Your #Hell.
Be Persuaded.
#drMM

SON71 #DearSon
If Passion, Real AND Kind Arrive...

In Same Package...*Linger.*
It's Almost *Irreplaceable,* Son.
#drMM

SON72 #DearSon
#Desire Is...Not A #*Divine* #Instruction.
(You Will Even See Deadly Things...*Inviting.*)
#Dad@64.
#drMM

SON73 #DearSon
Captivity...
Is The #*Enemy* of #Love.
#drMM

SON74 #DearSon
#Meanness...
Only Excites *Perverted.*
#Kindness...Is *Intoxicating.*
Wait For Her *Aroma,* Son.
She's Worth Waiting For.
#drMM

SON75 #DearSon
She Labors Hard...For $ponsor$hip.
She Labors Not...For #Credibility.
#drMM

SON76 #DearSon
Are Your Conversations About Your Dreams...or
Her Bills..?
Duh. #drMM

SON77 #DearSon
Your #Wife…
Creates
#*Energy.*
#drMM

SON78 #DearSon
Your #Wife…
Creates
#*Motivation.*
#drMM

SON79 #DearSon
Do You Really Enjoy Her…
When You Do Not
Have A Need..?
#drMM

SON80 #DearSon
No #Woman *Respects* The #Man…
She Has Mastered.
Real or Perceived.
Ever.
#drMM

SON81 #DearSon
Those Who Achieve *Little*…
Rarely Admire Those
Who Have Achieved *Much.*
#drMM

SON82 #DearSon
She Is Turning This Into Quite A *Chase*.
Her Thrill May Be *Stalkers*.
Give Her A Few Years of Freedom.
Dad.
#drMM

SON83 #DearSon
Her *Preparation* For Time With You...
Explains How She *Values* You.
(Queen of Sheba/Solomon)
Abigail/David)
#drMM

SON84 #DearSon
If She *Bores* You At Dinner...
Why Keep Her For A #Lifetime..?
#drMM

SON85 #DearSon
Her #*Reaction* To Your Request...
Explains Your #World She Would Create For You.
#drMM

SON86 #DearSon
Continuously Compare
YOUR #Investment In The #Relationship...
With Hers...*Continuously*.
($/Time/Energy)
Shocking.
#drMM

SON87 #DearSon
#The_Right_One...
Will Love *Learning* From You.
The Wrong One...
Loves *Correcting* You.
#*Decision* Is Easy.
#drMM

SON88 #DearSon
What Is Her Investment...In Your Dreams..?
#drMM

SON89 #DearSon
You Lost Her To The Court Jester.
Her Need For His Jovial Jesting Exceeded Her
Need For Your Wisdom.
#drMM

SON90 #DearSon
#The_Right_One Is...Not Necessarily "Ready."
Are You..?
The Greater The #Training...
The Greater The Future.
#drMM

SON91 #DearSon
Never Stop The Flow of Her Anger;
It Contains Too Many Secrets.
#drMM

SON92 #DearSon
#The_Right_One...Wants To Know Your #Wisdom.

The Wrong One...Wants To Know Your
#Weakness.
(Delilah/Queen of Sheba)
#drMM

SON93 #DearSon
Her Request...Revealed Her Perception of You.
...Money Bags
...Sugar Daddy
...Fool.
#Dad@64.
#drMM

SON94 #DearSon
When Her Affection Accompanies Her
Request...You Have Just Entered The Web of
The Spider.
#Dad@64.
#drMM

SON95 #DearSon
The Spider Is Discerned...Last.
#drMM

SON96 #DearSon
Attention Is...Quite A Gift;
Her Reaction To It Should Be Analyzed Before
You Offer Another #Gift.
#drMM

SON97 #DearSon
#The_Right_One...Will Discern You, Too~

Unless...
You Have Been Asking God...For His Most
Ignorant.
#drMM

SON98 #DearSon
If You Don't LOVE #Conversation With Her...God
Has Answered You.
Unmistakably.
#drMM

SON99 #DearSon
The #Fool...Will Study Her Walk.
The Wise...Will Study Her Work.
#drMM

SON100 #DearSon
Her Ability To Discern...Will Remove Your Need
To Persuade.
#drMM

SON101 #DearSon
When You See What Excites Her...You Will
Understand Why She Does Not ExciteYou.
#drMM

SON102 #DearSon
#The_Right_One...May Need You.
The Right One...Will Heed You.
The Difference Is Your #Heaven or Hell.
#drMM

SON103 #DearSon
Enjoying Her Is...Not Proof You Can Fulfill Her.
#drMM

SON104 #DearSon
What Excites Her...Your Attention or Your
#Admiration?
That Makes #Decision-Making Very Easy.
#drMM

SON105 #DearSon
The Bait Used...Explains Her Perception of You.
#Dad@64.
#drMM

SON106 #DearSon
#The_Right_One...Unlocks An Unexplainable
#Passion To Share Your Secrets.
The Wrong One...Evokes Caution.
#drMM

SON107 #DearSon
Her #Love For You Is...Exciting/Exotic.
But, Are You REALLY In Love With Her..?
There's Your Answer.
#drMM

SON108 #DearSon
If She Thinks A #Conversation Is A Date...She
Will Think A Kiss Is A Proposal.
(Slow The River Down.)
#drMM

SON109 #DearSon
You Don't Ache At The Thought of Seeing Her
With Someone Else?
She Is NOT..."The One."
#drMM

SON110 #DearSon
I Knew She Wasn't #The_Right_One When I Told
Her, "I Really Want #God To Bring The Right
Man To You."
And, I Meant It.
#drMM

SON111 #DearSon
Is She A 30-Minute Diversion...or A Lifetime
#Confidante?
#drMM

SON112 #DearSon
Study Her Well.
She Will Rule The World of Your #Mind.
The Rest of Your Life.
#drMM

SON113 #DearSon
Her Clothes...Explain Her #Goals.
Her #Words...Explain Her History.
Her #Friends...Explain Her Taste.
#drMM

SON114 #DearSon
You Are Concerned That Her Appearance Is...So

Invitational.
But, At Least Her Agenda Is Not Hidden.
:)
#drMM

SON115 #DearSon
Never #Trust Someone Who Does Not #Love You.
Never.
#drMM

SON116 #DearSon
Her #Disinterest In Your #Crisis...Explains Her
Heart. She Just Made Your #Decision Easier.
#drMM

SON117 #DearSon
When You See Who She Enjoys...You Won't Feel
So Special.
#drMM

SON118 #DearSon
Are You Silent About Your Greatest
#Problems...When With Her?
She Is NOT..."The One."
#drMM

SON119 #DearSon
I Noticed~When She Walks...Your Eyes Are Glad.
But_When She Talks...Your Eyes Are Sad.
Just Thinking.
Dad.
#drMM

SON120 #DearSon
Are You Becoming
Her...
...Confidante?
...Prayer Partner?
...Babysitter?
...Cry Towel?
...Sugar_Daddy?
You Know.
#drMM

SON121 #DearSon
What Is Her Reaction To~
...Your Achievements?
...Your Requests?
...Your Concerns?
...Your Counsel?
...Your Gifts?
#drMM

SON122 #DearSon...
The #Woman Who Does Not Solve Your
#Problems...Will Become Your Problem.
#drMM

SON123 #DearSon
Are Her Answers...Evasive?
Is Her Past...Unclear?
Are Her Requests...Inappropriate?
Is Her Mood...Unpredictable?
#drMM

`SON124` #DearSon
Is Her Focus...
...Her Knowing YOU?
or
...You Knowing HER?
Therein, Lies Your Answer.
Completely.
#drMM

`SON125` #DearSon
Does She...INSPIRE You?
How?
To~
...Think?
...Talk?
...Learn?
...Pray?
...Create?
...Excel?
...Honor?
...Listen?
#drMM

`SON126` #DearSon
Tell Me 4 Ways Her Presence Has Improved...
...Your Joy
...Your Finances
...Your Productivity
...Your Health.
#drMM

SON127 #DearSon
Do You Love Her...or The Feelings She Creates?
#drMM

SON128 #DearSon
When Do You Feel Caution With Her..?
Discussing~
...Your Fears?
...Your Financial Secrets?
...Your Sexual Needs?
#drMM

SON129 #DearSon
This IS Her...At Her Best.
She Is Investing What She Believes You Will
Accept.
Do You Feel Fortunate or Used?
#drMM

SON130 #DearSon
The Wrong One Will Cost You...For A Lifetime.
#The_Right_One...Costs A Little More Waiting.
#Dad@64.
#drMM

SON131 #DearSon
If She Doesn't Trust Your Decisions~She Will
Feel Unsafe.
If She Feels Unsafe~She Will Confide In Another.
#drMM

SON132 #DearSon
Her Reactions...Reveal Her Wisdom.
Her Mentors...Reveal Her Trust.
Her Tone...Reveals Her Honor.
#Dad@64.
#drMM

SON133 #DearSon
You Won't Survive A Marriage To Any
Woman...Who Distrusts Your #Decision-Making.
I Warned You.
#Dad@64.
#drMM

SON134 #DearSon
#Integrity...Invites Inspection.
#Deception...Acts Insulted By It.
#drMM

SON135 #DearSon
Her Attraction...May Not Be Caused By Her
Greatness.
Attraction May Be Caused By...Your Weakness.
#drMM

SON136 #DearSon
If Your Counsel Is Ignored...So Will Your Needs
Be.
#drMM

DECISION

Will You Accept Jesus As Your Personal Savior Today?

The Bible says, "That if thou shalt confess with thy mouth the Lord Jesus, and shalt believe in thine heart that God hath raised Him from the dead, thou shalt be saved," (Romans 10:9).

Pray this prayer from your heart today!

"Dear Jesus, I believe that You died for me and rose again on the third day. I confess I am a sinner...I need Your love and forgiveness...Come into my heart. Forgive my sins. I receive Your eternal life. Confirm Your love by giving me peace, joy and supernatural love for others. Amen."

CLIP AND MAIL

DR. MIKE MURDOCK

is in tremendous demand as one of the most dynamic speakers in America today.

More than 17,000 audiences in over 100 countries have attended his Schools of Wisdom and conferences. Hundreds of invitations come to him from churches, colleges and business corporations. He is a noted author of over 250 books, including the best sellers, *The Leadership Secrets of Jesus* and *Secrets of the Richest Man Who Ever Lived.* Thousands view his weekly television program, *Wisdom Keys with Mike Murdock.* Many attend his Schools of Wisdom that he hosts in many cities of America.

☐ Yes, Mike, I made a decision to accept Christ as my personal Savior today. Please send me my free gift of your book, *31 Keys to a New Beginning* to help me with my new life in Christ.

NAME _____ BIRTHDAY _____

ADDRESS _____

CITY _____ STATE   ZIP _____

PHONE _____ EMAIL _____ DFC

Mail to: **The Wisdom Center** · 4051 Denton Hwy. · Ft. Worth, TX 76117
1-817-759-BOOK · 1-817-759-2665 · 1-817-759-0300
You Will Love Our Website..! WisdomOnline.com

DR. MIKE MURDOCK

1 Has embraced his Assignment to Pursue...Proclaim...and Publish the Wisdom of God to help people achieve their dreams and goals.

2 Preached his first public sermon at the age of 8.

3 Preached his first evangelistic crusade at the age of 15.

4 Began full-time evangelism at the age of 19, which has continued since 1966.

5 Has traveled and spoken to more than 17,000 audiences in over 100 countries, including East and West Africa, Asia, Europe and South America.

6 Noted author of over 250 books, including best sellers, *Wisdom for Winning, Dream Seeds, The Double Diamond Principle, The Law of Recognition* and *The Holy Spirit Handbook.*

7 Created the popular *Topical Bible* series for Businessmen, Mothers, Fathers, Teenagers; *The One-Minute Pocket Bible* series, and *The Uncommon Life* series.

8 The Creator of The Master 7 Mentorship System, an Achievement Program for Believers.

9 Has composed thousands of songs such as "I Am Blessed," "You Can Make It," "God Rides On Wings of Love" and "Jesus, Just The Mention of Your Name," recorded by many gospel artists.

10 Is the Founder and Senior Pastor of The Wisdom Center, in Fort Worth, Texas...a Church with International Ministry around the world.

11 Host of *Wisdom Keys with Mike Murdock,* a weekly TV Program seen internationally.

12 Has appeared often on TBN, CBN, BET, Daystar, Inspirational Network, LeSea Broadcasting and other television network programs.

13 Has led over 3,000 to accept the call into full-time ministry.

THE MINISTRY

1 **Wisdom Books & Literature** - Over 250 best-selling Wisdom Books and 70 Teaching Tape Series.

2 **Church Crusades** - Multitudes are ministered to in crusades and seminars throughout America in "The Uncommon Wisdom Conferences." Known as a man who loves pastors, he has focused on church crusades for over 43 years.

3 **Music Ministry** - Millions have been blessed by the anointed songwriting and singing of Mike Murdock, who has made over 15 music albums and CDs available.

4 **Television** - *Wisdom Keys with Mike Murdock,* a nationally-syndicated weekly television program.

5 **The Wisdom Center** - The Church and Ministry Offices where Dr. Murdock speaks weekly on Wisdom for The Uncommon Life.

6 **Schools of The Holy Spirit** - Mike Murdock hosts Schools of The Holy Spirit in many churches to mentor believers on the Person and Companionship of The Holy Spirit.

7 **Schools of Wisdom** - In many major cities Mike Murdock hosts Schools of Wisdom for those who want personalized and advanced training for achieving "The Uncommon Dream."

8 **Missions Outreach** - Dr. Mike Murdock's overseas outreaches to over 100 countries have included crusades in East and West Africa, Asia, Europe and South America.

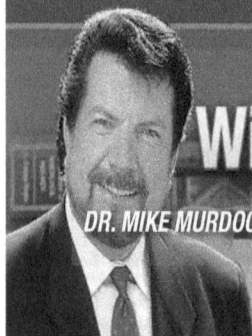

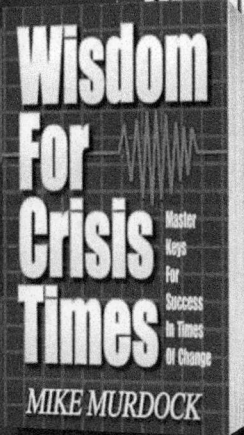

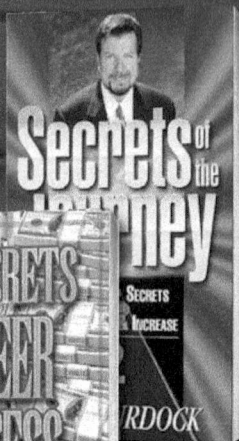

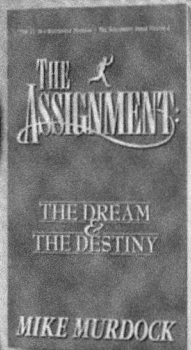

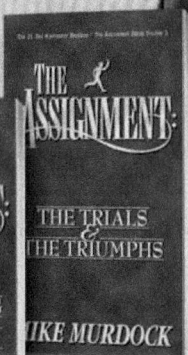

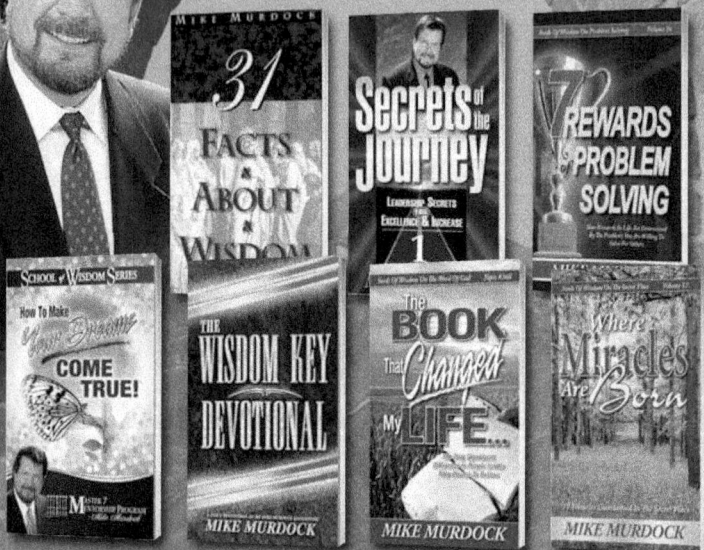

www.ingramcontent.com/pod-product-compliance
Lightning Source LLC
Chambersburg PA
CBHW060643030426
42337CB00018B/3423